The New Romantics

the art of musical divination

by: Ayesha Ophelia

WILDROSE PUBLISHING. 2024

honorable mentions.

for as long as sound has existed, so has romance...

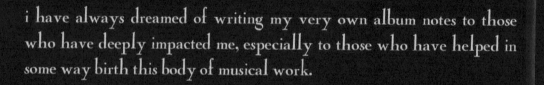

the
new
romantics

i have always dreamed of writing my very own album notes to those who have deeply impacted me, especially to those who have helped in some way birth this body of musical work.

to my mom, angela ophelia, there is not a day that passes that doesn't in some way contain you. thank you for showing up so fiercely, consistently, and lovingly (in life and in death). it's true! every story is about the mother. to my father, michael meriweather, an inspiration to me: who is the poetic embodiment of the romantic heart.

to my brothers (and amber) who form the
meriweather tribe i extend gratitude for the heart
expanding and complex journey of choosing to be
siblings. to my first love and one of my greatest teachers
zachary: love is so big it can contain all things, even endings.
and to sky 'mcswain' whom my future belongs to: let's set sail and
adventure all of our days. to all my friends near and far who have
supported, loved, and encouraged me: i will carry you into every lifetime
after this. and for the true romantics holding this book: may each word
bring the blessings of deep inner knowing, possibility, beauty, and inner
and outer revolution!

xo,

Ayesha Ophelia

6

The nature of the individual human spirit is one of romance, we humans are all really poets, pirates and lovers.

Richard Rudd

LOVE NOTES FOR
THE NEW ROMANTICS

"Romance is often written off as 'superfluous' (by those who have clearly never experienced it's power + magic) so Ayesha Ophelia, in a way that ONLY Ayesha Ophelia can, reminds us, through this delicious combination of sound, oracle, science + sensorial pleasure, that the frequency of romance is, has, + forever will be, a major force for change + is absolutely required for revolutions + evolutions.
It's a poetic love note, it's a spiritual transmission AND it's a magical support system to help us all remember what really matters, that romancing the whole of life is how we shift paradigms + create an entirely new vision to re-shape reality. "
Lisa Lister, artist, seer + bestselling author of Witch, Code Red + Self Source-ery

"Ayesha Ophelia's new book inspires a romantic renaissance of hope and transformation. For anyone seeking to see the worlds of beauty hidden within this world, her writing is an invitation to fall in love with this moment, this lifetime, and the sweetness of possibilities that are just waiting to be discovered. Especially for music lovers and musicians, this guidebook attunes us with sacred listening. One song at a time it moves us sonically deeper. Prepare to dance beyond the surface of sound toward divine divination and interconnectivity. "
Valerie June Hockett, Grammy nominated artist from Tennessee is a poet, author, and certified yoga and mindfulness meditation instructor

"The New Romantics is a masterful, imaginative, and compelling original divination system created by the amazing Ayesha Ophelia. Combining her personal story with music, beautiful collage art, the sacred science of music, a toe dip into the power of the renaissance times, which we are in, and a how-to turn your musical collection into an oracle, she bridges worlds as only she could. "
Colette Baron-Reid is a world-renowned Intuitive Counselor, Psychic Medium, TV Personality, Oracle deck creator, Author and Radio Show Host

"Ayesha Ophelia's "The New Romantics" is a groundbreaking exploration of sound, divination, and the transformative power of music. As a woman deeply committed to empowering individuals to find their strength, inner sight and voice, I am thrilled to see Ayesha's journey into the sacred ancestral science of divination. The New Romantics core magic lies in the practice of shufflemancy using the shuffle function of a playlist as a means to divine messages, insights, and guidance. Her novel approach transforms any playlist into a dynamic oracle system, which Ayesha aptly names "sound decks". This unique system invites us into a world where music becomes a bridge to the Divine, a tool for insight, and a catalyst for personal and collective change. Ayesha's approach of turning playlists into powerful sound decks for divination is a testament to her creative genius and a gift to all seeking new ways to connect with the Divine and our inner selves. "

Abiola Abrams, Creatrix of the African Goddess Rising Oracle and Secrets of the Ancestors Oracle, and founder of Womanifesting.com

"Ayesha Ophelia is the muse incarnate. A whirlwind of creativity, courage and learning, she is unparalleled. The New Romantics is a call to live freely and fiercely! Enticing, deep and interwoven, this musical divination journey introduces us to ourselves, and the universe around us. Ayesha opens a path to the miraculous here, a key to the code of our deepest satisfaction. A true work of the visionary, this is the magic that births new worlds."

Alexandra Love is a spiritual coach, meditative guide, sound healing musician in Beautiful Chorus, writer and artist

A each track page has a circle.

like this

B inside that circle is a song suggestion.

C feel free to play the song just before, after or during your reading of this guidebook.

FOR THE RECORD VOL. 1

AYESHA OPHELIA · SONG ORACLE QUESTIONS

MONO · SIDE A

The New Romantics

Wild Hearts Records

DECK SOLD SEPERATELY

side a

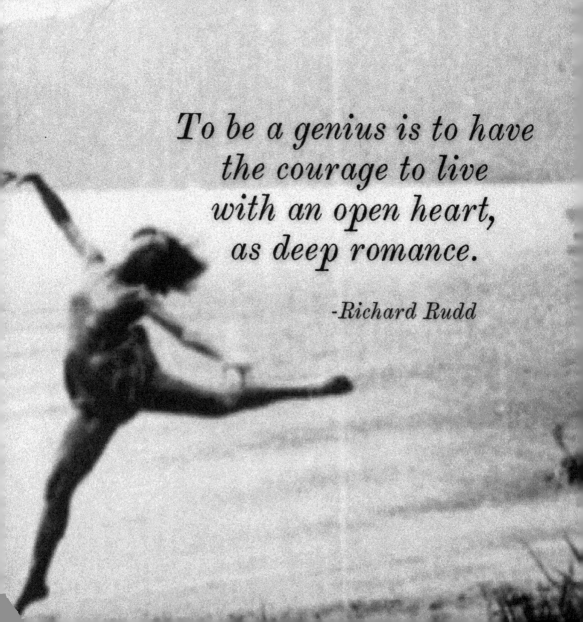

To be a genius is to have
the courage to live
with an open heart,
as deep romance.

-Richard Rudd

The New Romantics Tracklist

SIDE A

(intro) prelude to a kiss

01. the universe is a cosmic sound

02. the ancient roots of divination

03. for the record

SIDE B

04. song oracle system

05. creativity in seeking the unseen

06. (outro) living as a seer

MENDELSSOHN
Symphony No. 4 in
A major, Op. 90
"Italian" I
Allegro Vivace

intro. prelude to a kiss

SOUND
IS AN ORGANIZATION OF LOVE TEMPORARILY CRYSTALLIZED.
SOLOMON FESSHAYE

It takes a certain kind of mind to entertain the idea that romance is a necessary energy for evolution. The people I admire most seem to be capable of understanding romance at more than just face value. They are able to look beneath the surface and find the winding roots of romance. Flowers lure us in with their fragrance and beauty only to reveal the deeper presence we have been lacking in just a moment of pausing to appreciate the mesmeric beauty of a bloom. That is why we often use the old adage about stopping to smell the roses. It holds a deep truth about the kinship between humans and nature.

Romance draws us into a portal of hidden possibilities, revealing itself when we pause to be enraptured by the beauty of flowers. The dictionary definition emphasizes a key element, using the word ‹supernatural› to define romance, suggesting an exciting and mysterious quality. This points us toward the depth of romance, beyond mere excitement, and deeper into the supernatural mystery associated with love and life.

This body of work was called into my experience through the spirit of romance. The New Romantics guidebook will show you how to use music as an oracle and will reveal the steps in my divination system as well as explore the mechanics of oracular wisdom told through the art and sacred science of sound. Each track will be speckled with my own numinous and personal experiences with song and sound.

WHERE ROMANCE FLOURISHES, HEARTS UNITE!

To grasp the essence of The New Romantics, we must journey back to the paradoxical Renaissance eras before progressing forward into the practice of musical divination.

Think of me as your resident free spirit, here to remind you that romance matters. One might think that an invitation to remember romance is naive or misdirected in times such as these. The kind of romance I'm speaking of is the kind of cosmic energy that births worlds. This is more a matter of quantum physics and the mysterious nature of reality than romantic comedies or syrupy sweet gestures for loved ones. Although romance also manifests in the world as beauty, poetry, love, seduction, the art of language, and ultimately as thought patterns that collectively move humanity forward into new realms of possibility.

The essence of romance is an extremely powerful life-giving sensual force for change. I view the romantic periods in our history as cycles of time where the artists, ignitors, and outliers brought the collective lens to matters of the heart, the spiritual potential of creativity, and the continued awakening of consciousness. Music, literature, beauty, and artistic expression were the channels for this new frequency to move into the lifeblood of cultures.

The unexplainable, the euphoric, the awe-inspiring would unearth the template for discoveries on the shimmering horizon. The hearts of the people tuned towards enchantment and possibility instead of fear and control will always create a ripple of potentiality in time.

The term "Renaissance", meaning rebirth, in French, is often associated with Romanticism, a movement that perpetually challenges purely rational paradigms. Romantics seek to expand the widely accepted view of who we are and what is possible when humanity loses sight of the familiar shorelines of reality and ventures into new and mysterious waters.

At the heart of Romantic periods, there was a natural pulling away from political and social constraints. Romantics are imaginative people who champion creativity, natural beauty, artistic freedom, and soul exploration. This is exactly how life is approached when we remember that new things need space to grow and emerge in our collective consciousness. At its heart, romance is the dropping of the veil, leaving behind the way things have been for the promise of what could be. It's a willingness to leap into the void of creation with trust despite the lack of evidence. The Romantics became the evidence!

During these fertile times, cultural movements and new pieces of art were created that served as a catalyst to open the hearts and minds of humanity. This was one of the original times of 'freeing the nipple' and it meant exposure of not just breasts as a sign of how fertile a woman was. I see it also as a metaphor for the ways in which one must become naked to truly allow for anything new to thrive. This is the magical quantum sphere where romance returns us to the ever pervasive mystery.

ROMANCE, MEET DESTINY!

It's no surprise that divinatory arts exploded during these times. Enough people desiring in unison creates an opening for the cosmos to "show her hand" a little more.

Romantic periods fostered "a growing popular interest in mysticism, alchemy, and the occult, and hundreds of texts were published on such topics as the Kabbalah, Gnosticism, and alchemical applications in medicine. Witchcraft, magic, and divination were practiced in various forms, and astrological theories were disseminated in almanacs and horoscopes. People of all social ranks participated in rituals and séances to connect with the supernatural."
Paul O'Brien

Delving into the intricacies of this era unveils the foundation behind The New Romantics divination system, born from the fusion of romance, mystery, and music. Flirting with the captivating yet turbulent Renaissance periods provides insight into seeing beauty amidst chaos. This understanding enables us to perceive current turbulent times as an essential catalyst fostering revolutionary ideas and pivotal global transformations.

In the time of the Romantics, music became a living, breathing energy of alchemy. Classical composers began to allow their emotions and imagination to lead them to a new array of composing possibilities. Listeners would be taken on a mythical musical journey where once stale notes with little feeling were now imbued with life through passion, possibility, despair, and finally a bountiful overflowing hope.

The Romantic periods were prolific for culture and spirituality as it is known and experienced today. Without the romantic periods, we wouldn't have Frankenstein by Mary Shelly, the art and resistance of Frida Kahlo, ‹Les Misérables›, the poetry of William Blake, the dark and edgy Edgar Allen Poe, the revolutionary words of Zora Neale Hurston, the militant and direct voice of Marcus Garvey, the surreal Salvador Dali, the original pussy painter Georgia O'Keeffe, and so many more. I invite you to bring to mind some people known and unknown who fit the archetype of the romantic. I have also included some of my favorite pattern interrupters of my generation who carry the essence of the romantics in their blood, people like, Saul Williams, Ai Weiwei, Lisa Bonet (the patron saint of The New Romantics), Daniel Johnston, Octavia Butler, Tupac, Jean-Michel Basquiat, Bob Marley, Tim Burton, James Baldwin, Cindy Sherman, Jim Carrey, Russell Brand, Devendra Banhart, Wes Anderson, Maya Angelou, Richard Rudd, Valerie June, Jeff Goldblum, and perhaps you if you are drawn to a book such as this.

The romantic periods know no cultural boundaries. Every nation, region, and time are all at the effects of romance, which is an evolutionary energy seeded within humanity to ensure our success as a species.

"Romanticism was a "shift away from thinking of the universe as a static mechanism, like a clock, to thinking of it as a dynamic organism, like a growing tree....For those who make the shift, the values of static mechanism—reason, order, permanence, and the like—are replaced by their counterparts in an organic universe—instinct or intuition, freedom, and change. Romantic thought is relativistic and pluralistic; it rejects absolute values, formal classifications, and exclusive judgments; it welcomes novelty, originality, and variety. It is less interested in distinctions than in relationships, particularly in the organic relationship which it posits between man and nature, or the universe, and (less often) between the individual and society. The great chain of being is replaced by an indefinitely extended and complicated live network of connecting filaments, as in the vascular system of a plant or in a mass of animal nerve tissue, by which every phenomenon is tied by countless direct and indirect contacts to every other.

When a new fact appears, it is not just another link in the chain or cog in the machine; it is an evidence of organic growth and development, and its emergence changes every previously existing aspect of the universe. A new characteristic is evidence of a totally new and different world. Therefore a romantic artist will strive, not to imitate an ideal perfection of form which has always existed, but to originate a form which has never existed before and which will uniquely express what he alone feels and knows. To do so, he will rely more on imagination than on logic, more on symbols than on signs or allegories, more on unconscious than on conscious powers. He will believe that he is creating a genuinely new thing and thereby changing and renewing the whole of his organic universe."

Richard P. Adams

We are now entering another phase of the renaissance cycle. The New Romantics of the 20th century are being called upon to ground into a whole new frequency of possibility. The New Romantics are visionary dreamers and pioneers of our time, liberating themselves from mainstream mandates and the controlling establishments of governments and other structures that seek to suppress or conceal ancient wisdom. Instead, romantics are delving into the far reaches of their spirits, hearts, and imagination. I salute the courageous ones who keep an open heart in the midst of chaos. You are the harbingers, the bridge builders of a new Earth.

Of utmost importance to the written word in your hand is the idea that during the Romantic periods, humanity collectively begins to look more deeply within themselves for some of life's big answers. It's as if the seed that was planted before birth is finally ready to push through the soil into the light. The desire to bloom causes humans to seek for tools that enable deep inner knowing beyond the five senses. Romantics are thirsting for a kind of numinous experience that opens up new avenues, healing modalities, and ways of understanding who we are and why we are here.

The New Romantics guidebook is an exploration of possibility, music, divination, and healing in a ‹mixtape› collage style of writing and art. It is meant to accompany my oracle deck called ‹‹For The Record.››

As you journey on I will begin to refer to my music divination technique as ‹the song oracle›. Chapters are called tracks to stick with the musical undertones of The New Romantics. In addition, you'll discover inspiration, quotes, spaces for notes, and insights into your own intuitive, romantic heart. You'll also learn my precise technique for engaging with sound as a living, breathing oracular energy.

Take heed: These pages are intended to be encountered as poetry. To fully embrace this experience, you are encouraged to shift into your feeling body, which is also referred to as the emotional or spiritual body. You will know when you have arrived here because your breathing will shift and you will enter the softer space of the heart and soul. Hard edges, harsh conclusions, and rigid boundaries relax and blur in this realm, allowing for a more intuitive and holistic experience of the text. Allow yourself to linger in the pauses between words, to feel the rhythm of the sentences as they ebb and flow like music that only your soul can hear. In this way, you can truly immerse yourself in the essence of these pages, letting the poetry speak to you in its own language of the heart. This body of work is an invitation to return to the rapturous sublime energy of potential that sets all of life in motion.

THE TERM Selah IS FOUND IN THE HEBREW BIBLE AND IS THOUGHT TO BE A MUSICAL NOTATION OR DIRECTION, THOUGH ITS EXACT MEANING IS UNCERTAIN. IT'S OFTEN INTERPRETED AS A PAUSE OR A MUSICAL INTERLUDE, SUGGESTING A MOMENT OF REFLECTION OR MEDITATION. TAKE A SACRED SELAH AND LISTEN TO LAURYN HILL'S SONG CALLED SELAH.

The sublime was an experience whereby one views an object so beautiful and astonishing that we are unable to hold anything else in mind. Experiencing the sublime is more than the experience of beauty. Instead, it is to experience something so awe-inspiring that it overtakes our sense of objective reality.

Isabella Meyer

My bright hope is that the spirit of all romantics will create a new ethos for humankind to exist within. One where more possibility, more beauty, more bravery, more love, more connection, and more ability to move through the inevitable tough stuff is awakened. Romantics channel their energy into creating the new rather than battling the old, rendering the old system obsolete, as romantic, Buckminster Fuller aptly reminds us.

ode to romantics

May the bridges you burn light the way.
May the sounds you find hold deep insight.
May romance become a deeper contemplation.
May your heart be allured into embracing
ever-expanding possibilities.
May we live more romantic lives!

love,
the break...
of your
soul
upon
my lips

take the quiz.

ARE YOU A

ROMANTIC?

Take this quiz to find out if you have the spirit of a romantic
For every yes count 1 point.

1. Do you often find yourself prioritizing emotion over reason ?

2. Do you value individuality and uniqueness in people ?

3. Are you drawn to expressing your personal emotions through art, writing, or other creative outlets ?

4. Do you feel a strong connection to nature and find it spiritually inspiring ?

5. Have you ever experienced a sense of awe and wonder when contemplating natural landscapes ?

6. Are you captivated by the grandeur and beauty of the natural world ?

7. Do you enjoy exploring fantastical or otherworldly themes in literature, art, or entertainment ?

8. Is your imagination a significant part of your creative process or problem-solving ?

9. Have you ever been drawn to the supernatural or the mysterious ?

10. Do you feel a sense of nostalgia or longing for a simpler, less industrialized way of life?

11. Are you concerned about the impact of urbanization and industrialization on the environment and human society?

12. Do you value craftsmanship and the preservation of traditional arts and crafts?

13. Do you believe in the transformative power of love and passion?

14. Have you ever experienced love as an intense, all-consuming emotion?

15. Do you view love as a central theme in art, literature, and life?

16. Do you feel a strong connection to your cultural heritage and traditions?

17. Are you interested in the folklore, myths, and legends of your own culture or others?

18. Do you believe in celebrating and preserving cultural diversity but in a none woke virtue signaling way?

19. Do you believe in challenging established norms and institutions when they are unjust?

20. Do you feel a sense of responsibility to work toward positive change in society?

21. Are you fascinated by historical periods and drawn to historical novels or films?

22. Do you believe that understanding history is essential for shaping the future?

23. Have you ever found inspiration in the art, literature, or philosophy of past eras?

24. Do you feel a sense of wonder when contemplating the mysteries of the universe?

25. Have you ever sought to transcend everyday life through spiritual practices or artistic expression?

26. Do you believe in the pursuit of ideals that point us to a better collective future?

Results

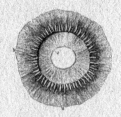

0 - 6 Blush of the poet

You find beauty in romantic ideals but it's still a growing flame.
To tend that flame let your life become a poem. Lose track of
time. Flirt with the universe.

7 - 13 Nature's Reverie

Nature's essence is deeply felt within. You mirror the untamed
beauty and boundless creativity found in the heart of the natural world. Remember nature is always calling you deeper into
romance.

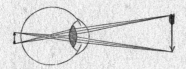

14 - 20 Eternal Dreamer

You love to explore the profound landscapes of human experience, wild nature, and the limitless realms of creativity. However to live as the romantic requires a daily devotion to the mystery. What will your romantic gesture be today?

21 - 26 New Romantic

Congrats you are a New Romantic through and through! You are here to help birth a new era of creative exploration and evolution. One where artists, minds oriented toward the future, poets, black sheep, and lovable misfits are the catalysts for revolutionary being.

the new romantics
basic principles

1. *Periods of chaos are classically what have helped to facilitate the birth of new spiritual technology.*

2. *Sound is a living, breathing energy with vast intelligence.*

3. *Romance is the desire of all things to exist before they manifest. It is the spark of desire that births worlds.*

4. *Divination is an ancient and accurate method of tapping into the invisible current that sustains the universe.*

5. *Sound is deeply healing and can alter your physiology on multiple levels.*

6. Sound is a quantum technology that will be studied, and mysteries will continue to be revealed over time.

7. Anyone is capable of working with sound and music as an oracle, not only to receive answers that lead to deeper healing but also to communicate beyond the veil to 'the other side'.

8. We are once again at a tipping point for humanity, and the energy we embody **now** will carry us into vast new possibilities.

9. The universe hides **many** secrets in plain sight.

TAKE NOTE.

A PLACE TO COLLECT YOUR ROMANTIC NOTIONS.

Perfectly
sized
to share
on Instagram stories.

1
2
3
4
5
6
7
8
9
10
11 ♥
12
13
14
15
16
17
18

"Today all sounds belong to a continuous field of
Possibilities lying within the comprehensive dominion
of music. Behold the new orchestra: the sonic universe!
And the musicians: anyone and anything that sounds!"
–R. Murray Schafer

Music is an unparalleled force on our planet, connecting all living
things. It heals, bridges borders, and initiates life. It offers beauty,
solace, and inner reflection, evoking deep feelings of all kinds and
providing immediate, perceptible feelings of healing in the body.
I believe sound can also offer us an infinite amount of information
as a divinatory tool.

A secret: even if our ears cannot perceive it, sound is always felt
through the feeling body, which is the part of ourselves connected
to deeper primal wisdom. All things create a sound, a vibration, a
signature of understanding.

"Music doesn't emerge from random creative inspiration. Songs
aren't chaos. Instead, they involve structure, pattern, repetition
and other characteristics that make them recognizable to the human
ear. In the end, music is a sort of science -- a fascinating, pulsating type of sound that peers through people's aural perceptions
and into the universe beyond. We humans have organs specifically
designed to detect and understand sound. Our fleshy ears snag all
sorts of sounds, from the chirping of crickets to the pounding of
jackhammers, to classical music streaming through radio signals."
-Nathan Chandler

We have been expertly designed to receive the frequency of music. It's as if the creator made us audio jacks for music to flow through. Music effortlessly interacts with us on a cellular level. For many of us, the notes wash over our bodies creating goosebumps of pleasure and deep recognition of something that stirs above the level of mind and resides deep in the regions of the soul.

As you explore the sacred science of sound in this track it is imperative to lead with your heart. The power of music divination cannot fully meet you if you are closed off to it. Listen up friends! The key advice here is to ditch those outdated notions about how the universe works and what's possible. Strap on your badge of curiosity (and non-judgment) if you dare to proceed!

curiously committed

to evolving

When you are extremely gifted you tend to notice patterns that many other people do not connect. Nikola Tesla who was a master pattern recognizer espoused that "if you want to find the secrets of the universe, think in terms of energy, frequency, and vibration."

The Fibonacci sequence, often referred to as the golden ratio, serves as the architect behind the organization of imperceptible elements into the visible spectrum of light. This divine ratio orchestrates the intrinsic beauty we witness in the patterns of flowers, the graceful forms of trees, the hypnotic expanse of oceans, and even the flesh that is covering your bones holds these sacred codes. If our senses were finely attuned, we might discern this pattern as a harmonic sound—a symphony reverberating through the unseen layers of existence.

Moreover, these unseen frequencies resonate in the intangible realms, like the wind's whispers, the transmission of radio waves, the subtle vibrations of healing frequencies, or the ubiquitous presence of Wi-Fi signals—elusive to our sight but ever-present in our modern lives, intertwining with our daily existence. Not all frequencies carry the same creative potential. It is up to you to select and attune yourself to the frequencies that resonate most

"All organisms are made out of atoms and molecules, which means literally every living thing is radiating energy and vibration. Every living thing on earth vibrates at its own level with its own sound, determined by the velocity of its frequency. Motion gener- ates frequencies and in turn, generates sound whether we are able

48

to hear it or not. Everything has a sound, and it's own level of vibration. The specific sound is determined by the velocity (frequency) of the movement. All organisms on this planet use vibration i.e., energy, as the primary means of communication. In its original condition vibration is inaudible and invisible, but in its first stage towards manifestation it becomes audible, and its next step is visible."
-Penny Wong

The profound impact of music's power is widely recognized in our scientifically oriented society, leading to the development of sound healing techniques. These methods have been utilized by the United States War Department since 1945. For those intrigued by unexplored realms of possibility, exploring declassified military documents could reveal insights into how sound is employed at the highest echelons.

SPOILER
ALERT

OUT OF BODY
EXPERIENCES ARE REAL!

If the organizations with the most money and influence in the world believe in music therapies I think we should all be very curious about the power of sound and how it could be beneficial to health, well-being, and vital and spiritual energy.

49

Music therapy is defined as "the clinical use of music to accomplish individualized goals such as reducing stress, improving mood and self-expression." - A T M A It is an evidence-based therapy well-established in the health community. "Music therapy experiences may include listening to music, singing, playing instruments, composing music, or listening to the lyrics and drawing connections to one's own life. Musical skills or talents are not required to participate. Music therapy may help you psychologically, emotionally, physically, spiritually, cognitively, and socially." - Cleveland Clinic

The documented benefits include:
- Lowering blood pressure.
- Improving memory.
- Enhanced communication and social skills through experiencing music with others.
- Self-reflection. Observing your thoughts and emotions.
- Reducing muscle tension.
- Self-regulation. Developing healthy coping skills to manage your thoughts and emotions.
- Increasing motivation.
- Managing pain.
- Increasing joy.

Music therapy has also proved to be beneficial with dementia, stroke, traumatic brain injuries, Parkinson's disease, Cancer, Autism spectrum disorder, mood disorders, anxiety disorders, learning disabilities, developmental disabilities, pain, and substance abuse disorders. If I were the one writing that rather clinical list it would include music and sound as a doorway to creativity, a powerful tool to tend to the health of the soul, and a way to tap into the quantum field to receive answers.

For those who want to go deeper, another rabbit hole to venture into that links science, the government, and sound is connected to the scale that most music is now played in. In a nutshell, many believe the scale for all music was changed from 432 Hz to 440 Hz purposely to put people in a dissonant frequency where control is more easily possible. Many studies have been done that show the dramatic difference of these frequencies in heart rate, breathing, and other bodily markers that are signs of stress or relaxation. As always do your own research but do us all a favor and make sure you listen to some "whistle-blowers" and veer off the path of what Google says is real. Expansion happens in the space between the known and the unknown. When disbelief is suspended it allows for a new truth to emerge and we experience ourselves as more of the multidimensional badasses we are!

"Many ancient musical instruments were constructed for 432 Hz tuning and before the mid-20th century, 432 Hz was the standard of instrumental tuning. Since then 440 Hz tuning has become the norm. The 432 Hz frequency resonates with the Schumann Resonance of 8 Hz and is known for its deeply calming and soothing effects. A recent double-blind study from Italy showed that music tuned to 432 Hz slows down the heart rate when compared to 440 Hz." -BetterSleep

The science of sound seeks to explain what humans intuitively know and feel about the powerful effects of music. Many great minds and teachings of the past also held music as a creative force capable of great, even supernatural, works.

"It has been proven that the frequency we listen to actually changes our brain's frequency through the auditory cortex, altering our emotions that trigger releasing hormones and chemicals with the ability to heal the body. Interestingly, The Greek god Apollo was the god of both music and medicine, Aesculapius was believed to cure mental disorders with songs. The great philosophers Plato and Aristotle believed that music affected the soul and emotions. The use of tuning forks is said to balance our energies and center us. Our modern-day musical (12-tone scale) is slightly out of sync from the ancient Solfeggio frequencies (6-tone scale) originally developed by a Benedictine monk, Guido d'Arezzo (c. 991 AD — c. 1050 AD), traditionally associated with sacred music such as the Gregorian Chants. The chants and their special tones were believed to impart spiritual blessings when sung in harmony. Each Solfeggio tone is comprised of a frequency required to balance your energy and keep your body, mind, and spirit in perfect harmony. Today, we know the Solfeggio scale as seven ascending notes assigned to the syllables Do-Re-Mi-Fa-So-La-Ti. The original scale was six ascending notes assigned to Ut-Re-Mi-Fa-Sol-La. The syllables for the scale were taken from a hymn to St. John the Baptist." —Penny Wong

ORIGINAL SIX SOLFEGGIO FREQUENCIES

- 396 Hz for liberating one from fear and guilt
- 417 Hz for facilitating change and undoing situations
- 528 Hz for miracles and transformations like D N A repair
- 639 Hz for relationships and reconnecting
- 741 Hz for getting solutions and expressing yourself
- 852 Hz for returning one to a spiritual order
- 963 Hz to create room for oneness and unity

THE MISSING THREE SOLFEGGIO FREQUENCIES

- 174 Hz for calming, grounding, pain relief
- 285 Hz for renewal of energy fields and rearrangement
- 963 Hz for divinity, pineal glands, activation of the third eye, spirit

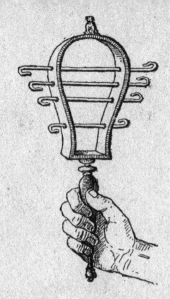

Sound healing is the practice of using audio tones and vibrational frequencies to repair damaged tissues and cells within the body. It works on the principle that all matter is vibrating at specific frequencies; and that sickness, disease, depression, and stress causes human beings to vibrate at a lower frequency.

SOUND HEALING AT HOME

SONG WORK

Pick the Solfeggio frequency you most need in your life and play it as you read along and move throughout your day. Note what changes in the moment and after weeks of listening.

EINSTEIN

Believes a Whole Description of 'the Physical Reality' Can Be Provided Eventually.

In quantum physics, entangled particles remain connected so that actions performed on one affect the other, even when separated by great distances.

The phenomenon so riled Albert Einstein he called it spooky action at a distance.

Karl Tate

"One of the most bizarre premises of quantum theory, which has long fascinated philosophers and physicists alike, states that by the very act of watching, the observer affects the observed reality." -Weizmann Institute of Science

Music and sounds exist as living entities, pulsating with life as intricate frequencies that traverse the invisible realms in waveforms. Within the study of quantum physics lies a principle known as "the observer effect", asserting that the act of observation inherently alters the observed phenomenon or situation. This concept breathes life into divination practices like the song oracle, where the very act of engaging in divination triggers a change of state.

When I consult my song oracle system for answers, my frequency aligns with a similar frequency in the musical realm. The song oracle is essentially the oracle within yourself, but experienced through the powerful and transformative lens of song. Each person's energy will interact with the system in a unique way, producing custom and individualized results.

If you cannot marry your belief in divinatory tools with my hypothesis of how the song oracle works, you can alternatively lean into the "feel-good-healing" of working with sound, that scientific studies back. Full disclosure, I don't know exactly how the whole thing works just as I cannot explain how many technologies we use on a daily basis work, but the song oracle system keeps showing me how unimportant knowing the exact mechanics are and how much more interesting it is to just believe and see what comes from the space of authentic asking.

I trust you will be a believer if you open up to possibility and follow the steps as well as your own intuition. The universe is a supremely mysterious organism and you don't have to have all the answers to receive many of the gifts of science, tech, mysticism, or spirituality.

Music is the mediator between the spiritual and the sensual life.

Ludwig van Beethoven

"Any sufficiently advanced technology is indistinguishable from magic." Arthur C. Clarke

I have personally ‹spoken› to loved ones ‹on the other side› about the process of dying through the song oracle. My Mom sent me a song that described her initial process of dying that gives me chills to this day. On the day a beloved family member tragically passed away by suicide, I sought answers by using the song oracle system. Astonishingly, shortly after learning of her passing, the system conveyed two songs that directly addressed the act of taking your own life.

Through ongoing experiments with the song oracle, I have fervently tested my hypotheses about using songs to connect beyond the veil, consistently encountering remarkable revelations. These experiences continually illuminate the multifaceted nature of our existence and our capacity to access profound knowledge and experiences beyond the constraints of conventional sensory understanding. I will share more about my experience connecting with loved ones ‹on the other side› in track 5.

For the skeptics and non-believers, consider this: electricity, Wi-Fi, and radio signals don›t require your belief to function. Every time I Airdrop something to a friend, I am further convinced of the unseen energetic frequencies that connect us all. The song oracle operates on the same principles.

BELIEF CHECKPOINT

For best results abandoning the need to know will increase the signal of the sound oracle. Curiosity is always the doorway through which mysteries flow.

Have you already encountered something in this guidebook that ignited fresh possibilities within you? Do you find yourself curious, eager to learn more? These are indications that the melodies are already resonating with you. In Track 4, you'll explore my complete song divination system. Additionally, the For the Record oracle deck (available separately) will guide you further into the realm of sound divination, also known as shufflemancy.

Do a quick sound experiment right now. Ask yourself, "What do I most need to know right now?". You now have two pathways of choice around receiving your oracle musical answer.

1. Wait until you know how to create a song deck to receive your first musical divination.
2. Go out into the world and see what songs just happen to be playing. This approach both involves a bit of flow and structure. Often, I recall my initial intention unexpectedly while a song is playing. Even though I might have heard numerous songs prior, the sudden recollection of my intention validates that the current song aligns with what I was seeking.

Art and science both render ideas about the world into a form that allows the viewer to connect to the idea. Lian Zhu

When art and science converge, magic unfolds. Children are conceived, concertos are written, and oracle systems are born. Synchronicities align according to an invisible yet divine plan. Your task isn't to comprehend precisely how all this unfolds; rather, it's to remain curious, open, and receptive to life's flow through you.

"Many scientists have found similarities between the structure of D N A and music. Parts of D N A and protein sequences are often repeated with very minor changes. This imperfect repetition has often been likened to the compositional structure of music, particularly classical music and music from the East. The idea that the human body itself is musical is not so far-fetched. We are a delicate framework of rhythms and melodies — our brainwaves, blood circulation, heartbeat, endocrine cycles and the very fluid of our cells all breathe according to a very consistent rhythm. At an even deeper subatomic level our molecules and their atomic structures also vibrate at very high frequencies and are designed around universal geometries. Seen in this way, the human being is nothing more than a symphony of interwoven rhythms, tempos and sounds." - Richard Rudd (Gene Keys)

Valerie June
Astral Plane

track 02

the ancient roots
of divination

"*Divination is not seeing the future; it's looking at the present from a different perspective and seeing connections that were otherwise invisible.*"

Charbel Tadros

Mancy: indicating   divination
of a particular kind.

The New Romantics

The profound enigmas of existence have forever urged humanity to seek answers. Deep within our intuitive selves, an invisible tether akin to an umbilical cord binds us to the mysteries of other realms, ensuring we never fully forget. It is from the space of inner inquiry that the divinatory arts arose, in harmony with—not apart from—the higher self.

I believe, as a species, our collective aspiration for evolution assists us in reconnecting with our multidimensional nature. We utilize an energetic blueprint that is sophisticated yet challenging for the logical mind to grasp, guiding us through life and aligning us with our soul. Some identify this as gut instinct, intuition, or synchronicity. Similar to nature's adaptive intelligence, which responds to current needs and challenges, we, too, are urged to explore beyond our boundaries for continued evolution, surpassing the wisdom of our oldest members in seeking new and innovative survival strategies.

Paul O'Brien wrote the book called "Divination: Sacred Tools for Reading the Mind of God". He was the man who held the vision for a new category of software in the late 80's, which would evolve to become the world's largest astrology and divination website. Here is a comprehensive gem from his book to help provide context to the many ways divination has evolved side by side with humans for millennia across all cultures.

foretell, intuition, predict, prophesy, forecast, foresee, prognosticate, forewarn, forebode, presume

"Human beings have always looked for the answers to life's great mysteries. Why are we here? Who controls our destiny? How does life work? What does the future hold? There is archeological evidence that a need to know and deep spiritual seeking are universal human traits, and that some form of divination has been used since the earliest times, to support this quest. Many cultures, including Chinese, Mayan, Mesopotamian and Indian, looked upwards to heavenly bodies— stars, planets, constellations, eclipses, and comets—not only to tell time and understand the seasons but also for signs of portent or to decipher changes attributable to divine action. Others paid special attention to terrestrial omens such as animal migrations and weather patterns, as well as patterns of tossed sticks, bones, amulets, or rocks. African tribes have used bones in divination rituals for hundreds of thousands of years. Chinese Taoists read patterns on tortoise shells, which evolved into the hexagrams of the I Ching. Vikings consulted the runestones. Ancient Roman shamans observed the entrails of slaughtered animals and grains that hens pecked at and formed messages (alectryomancy). Other cultures have looked to inner space (such as the Australian aborigines with their dreamtime), or have used entheogenic plants for vision quests (such as the Mazatec Indians of Mexico who use Salvia divinorum for spiritual rituals and divination). There are also numerous passages in the Old Testament documenting Jahweh's instructions for using a sacred set of dice called Urim and Thummim to make decisions in His name. Even though various forms of divination have been used in all societies, the widespread use of sophisticated divination systems across all classes

foretell, intuition, predict, prophesy, forecast, foresee, prognosticate, forewarn, forebode, presume

of people is a recent development. The spread of divination systems depended on oral transmission, which in preliterate times was largely the exclusive domain of the rulers, chieftains, official soothsayers, priests, sages, prophets and shamans. Although belief in magic was practically universal up to and through the Middle Ages, including primitive divinatory practices of folk magic, knowledge of divination systems and what Tarot scholar Bob O'Neill calls learned magic, could not spread until the invention of printing." —Paul O'Brien

Authentic divination systems passed down by our ancestors are a special type of heritage bestowed upon the human family. From a practical standpoint, divination systems can often provide a fresh perspective on the changing times and world, which is to our collective advantage. They also help us satisfy an ancient and instinctual need to better understand life and our place in the Universe.

The desire to look beyond the surface for meaning is reflected in this guidebook and through the song oracle as a tool for not only personal and planetary growth but also enjoyment, manifestation, healing, and the strengthening of your own intuitive abilities.

Divination can serve as a pathway to expand your consciousness, setting the stage for future generations to build upon. As you expand your beliefs, you are crafting an energetic blueprint within the quantum realm of potentiality. This process leads to the collective birth of tools that nurture spiritual growth in all of us.

There are thousands of types of divination and many of them are still practiced to this day around the globe. The suffix mancy means "divination by means of".

Biblomancy or Stichomancy is one of my favorite and most used forms of divination. I use this technique almost daily and invite you to use it with this very book since it involves an element of ‹fortune telling› or deep intuitive knowing with the use of printed books. It is one of the oldest forms of divination, believed to be at least 3000 years old, in which the querent opens to a random page of a book (often a holy book) to find an excerpt that applies to the question or quandary. The most common forms of this type of ‹mancy› are the ancient I Ching in which one consults the Chinese Book of Changes or Bibliomancy in which one consults the Bible or a similar book that has holy meaning. I use this same technique with any book I have around and routinely feel blown away by what I "randomly" pick.

Try it. See what paragraph or word first catches your eye as you open this book or another book nearby. Since most of my books are mystical or spiritual in nature, this practice has been incredibly enriching for me.

Divination has a long rich history that you are now a part of. By participating in the song oracle, using tarot, or creating a system of your own, you are written into the fabric of the divinatory arts. Your engagement strengthens the signal of possibility for everyone who is to come. You are now interacting as the oracle.

FRESHLY MINTED DIVINATORY WORDS *by Ayesha Ophelia*

* **MUSICDIVINOLOGY: DIVINATION THROUGH MUSIC.**

* **LYRICMANCY: DIVINATION THROUGH SONG LYRICS.**

* **SONNOMANCY: THE FIRST SONG HEARD IN A NEW PLACE SERVING AS A FORM OF DIVINATION OFFERING INSIGHT OR SYMBOLISM FOR THE TRAVELER'S JOURNEY OR EXPERIENCE IN THAT LOCATION.**

In esoteric thought, sound is seen as a gateway to altered states of consciousness. Drumming, chanting, and other rhythmic sounds are used in shamanic practices to induce trance states and spiritual journeys. The New Romantics is also a gateway into altered states of consciousness where more information is accessible beyond our perception, using the medium of music and divination.

Corinne
Bailey Rae
Put Your
Records On

track 03.

for the record

mélomanie

an inordinate liking for
music or melody

jacob banks nashville tn

For the record, music is hardwired into the double helix of my DNA. I can feel it living in my bones. I get the shivers listening to sounds. I see shapes and colors when certain music plays. I grew up hearing my Mom tell enchanted stories about my grandmother, Alyne Dumas Lee, who was a classically trained opera singer from Chicago. A series of fated and fortunate events saw to it that my grandmother would adopt two girls, one of which was my Mother, who, by destiny's design, was also a beautiful singer and would sing until her very last breath.

My music story begins here, in the ancestral waters of my mother's womb. My grandmother, Alyne Dumas Lee, from whom I inherited my middle name, not only had a giant heart but was also an acclaimed opera singer at the height of her career when she adopted my mom and her sister. She relocated to Alabama to be an adjunct teacher at a historically black Seventh Day Adventist college, where she continued her professional musical career and cared for her two new daughters until her passing.

listen to my grandma sing

75

The voices of these women are what shaped me into a person capable of knowing music as a living, breathing, conscious frequency. They held the medicine of sound deeply and passed the seed through me; first as a bud and now into a fuller bloom.

Many of my first memories as a child are connected to the force-field of music. My first vivid childhood recollection is of me lying on the floor in our living room with my favorite record at the time, which was of the 70s pop psychedelic Christian music flavor. The cover, which we can't display here without explicit copyright permission, was predominantly white. It featured a large wicker peacock chair, the one and only Reba looking serene with her hand on a stuffed white tiger, and delicate butterflies that reliably transported me into a musical universe. Even now, just glimpsing the cover starts to pull me out of the mundane world into a realm of imagination and possibility.

REBA
RAMBO
THE LADY IS A CHILD

Mixtape Memories: Musical Moments That Shaped Me

I was that kid in the choir who was enraptured by the music. My voice was never a soloist's but I thoroughly enjoyed spending my days and afternoons singing as an alto, sometimes second soprano, in the chorus. I sang in choirs throughout most of high school until it lost its appeal with me and my friends, so I quit. I then pursued other artistic interests and became obsessed with boys, design, creating magazine collages, making mixtapes, and crafting with my hands.

Church was another big source of music in my life. In church, I would imagine I was brave enough to be a handbell ringer in the front of the church. The bell ringers would wear white gloves and swing their bells to sweet gentle melodies about Jesus. When I would listen it would feel like an ancient code was unlocking.

I'd experience a completely different musical essence at the predominantly black churches my parents took us to where my Mom would sing and my dad would share poems and sermons. My soul felt like honey and I knew 'come what may' something had my back. The melodies, notes, and congregations willingness to be possessed by the spirit gave my musical experience roots and chaos and soul singing and goosebumps, every time! Gospel music became an avenue to know my ancestry through the vehicle of praise music in the Southern churches I would frequent with my parents.

Later, I had a big yellow tape player and it rarely left my side. Which then transformed into a Discman C D player, which later turned into an iPod, which encouraged me to begin a small collection of vinyl and cassettes, which later turned into an iPhone and finally into music streaming services. Now I use a little bit of all of these magical tools to commune with music.

Truthfully some of my favorite music can only be heard outside through the natural melodies that live on the tongues of birds, the howl of the wind or the wolves, and the melodic dissonance of the grasshoppers' song. Nature is a grand conductor of sound; fire crackles, river rush and hiss, and whales have haunting and ethereal choruses they sing underwater. Nature is the primal O M sound. The original source of music on the planet. Many traditions even believe music is what birthed the world into being.

I would be remiss to tell the story of my musical upbringing and not speak to the time in my life when I accrued the most prolific collection of music without spending a single penny. Do you remember the failed business model of 1 penny for 12 C Ds ? The paper invitation was in almost every magazine back when I was coming of age. I spent hours meticulously looking over the musical selections they printed, along with the no-postage-required postcard, to enter into an agreement for a certain number of regular-priced C Ds, none of which, in the history of ordering, anyone ever paid for. I share that many details because it was a turning point in my relationship with music. If this was a musical, it would be the part where the dramatic song plays over the montage of the main characters, foreshadowing at what is to come. In my case, a deep, abiding love affair with sound led me to create the song oracle system.

Thanks to the penny C Ds mixtapes, miniature soundtracks, became effortlessly crafted by ordinary individuals. They served as my personal musical mood ring during my teenage years. I curated these mixtapes not just for friends or crushes, but also as an outlet for emotions that found no other avenue of expression. This led to an explosion of music in all its forms. Music transformed into a sanctuary, a trusted confidant, and a guiding force.

In my twenties and early thirties, concerts became the backdrop of my life. It wasn't an out-of-the-ordinary occurrence to cross multiple state lines for a band or musician I loved. I stood in long lines, navigated mosh pits, and filled stadiums and small venues, experiencing firsthand the artists who had once only been names on my vast collection of C Ds. Often alone, often the only person who looked like me, it was the music that compelled me and kept calling me back. Through this dedication, I began to make friends with many of the musicians I had admired. Music has that power to connect kindred hearts.

As music became increasingly digital, I adapted. This is otherwise known as the "Spotify is my boyfriend" phase. The discover feature, which is just an algorithm or frequency that makes the user playlists based on your likes and music history, became a very used feature on my phone. This button was like finding the most intuitive lover and friend all in one. It also led me to some amazing new music and an insane amount of digital playlists created.

2015 was the year that I began playfully using my streaming service as an oracle. I would ask a question and see what the shuffle button would reveal. This would be the beginning of what has now turned into a full-fledged divination system. It was also around that time I self-published my own oracle deck and became extremely fascinated by divination and oracle systems.

A year or so into the song oracle experiment, I shared a snippet of the process on Instagram Stories and received an overwhelmingly positive and inquisitive response. Over the past few years, I've been romanced and wooed by the magic of streaming music and how it has become a trusted source of intuitive information as a divination system.

Sidenote: Like many music lovers who regularly use streaming services, I believe that these platforms have a long way to go in terms of providing more incentives and fair pay to creators. At the same time, I have to give major props because Spotify's streaming platform is where I discovered how to teach people to use sound as an oracle.

I share this meandering story of music in my life to paint a picture of how deeply intertwined music has been with every part of my life. My musical history undoubtedly laid the framework for the birth of the song oracle. We all have our unique story with music. Music is one of those forces of nature that can take us back to memories we had long tucked away.

Have you seen the trending video of the classically trained dancer with dementia? It shows her listening to music and being transported back to clear memories from her younger years. As she listens, she begins to sway, and her body, triggered by the sound, remembers the dance movements.

What are a few of your favorite music memories? We all have a patchwork of songs that will forever be a part of us, and for better or worse I'll be a woman in my 80s who knows the lyrics to Lil' Jon's love song "from the window to the wall."

HARMONIZING WITH THE SPIRIT OF MUSIC...

I would like to pay homage and honor all the other people who have created or worked with music as a system of divination. I certainly am not the first and won't be the last. You too shall be included in this sacred sound lineage just by using the song oracle.

"Music is a moral law. It gives a soul to the universe, wings to the mind, flight to the imagination, a charm to sadness, and life to everything. It is the essence of order, and leads to all that is good, just and beautiful, of which it is the invisible, but nevertheless dazzling, passionate, and eternal form"- Plato

side b

Music heard so deeply that is is not heard at all,
but you are the music while the music lasts.

T S Eliot

33 R.P.M.

Madama
Destiny
Written in
the Stars

track 04.

song oracle system

THE SONG ORACLE SYSTEM

The New Romantics' song oracle system is a form of shufflemancy. Just as one shuffles tarot cards or runes to seek guidance, shufflemancy here involves shuffling a playlist, or, as it's known here; a song deck. With a question posed, the answer reveals itself within the song that is randomly selected.

The song oracle is an ever-evolving library of music that you can use as a divination just as you would tarot or oracle cards. The process I will guide you through next is the same system I use to receive message from the other side, to tap into my own wisdom and intuition, and to ask questions that I need guidance with through the medium of music.

My invitation to you as a powerful creator is to make this system your own. Add bells, whistles, and ruminations that imbue the song oracle with your unique "magick". Nothing is set. Everything evolves.

I share the archaic spelling of magick as a wink and a nod to the more feminine or earthy style, distinct from stage magicians who master the art of illusion.

"Magick" is the various techniques used for harnessing internal and external energies that will help you change yourself or the environment around you, as opposed to magic which can be illusions like the rabbit in a hat trick. The New Romantics is 'magick' of the original kind.

How To:

The New Romantics Song Oracle System is a form of shufflemancy that consists of song deck creation, learning the art of asking amazing questions, and interpretation of songs. In the following track I will share some ways to build upon this basic system.

1. You will need to create a song deck using Spotify, Apple Music, Soundcloud, Pandora, iTunes collection of music, or another music streaming service.

2. To begin, I suggest having a playlist of 30-55 songs for your song deck. My main song oracle deck now includes thousands of songs to choose from. I also use smaller, specialized «decks» when I want to work with different energies. You can create multiple decks or playlists and curate them as you would a collection of oracle decks, with themes and names. Get creative and make song oracle decks based on your interests, desires, and curiosities. For example, if you're a love warrior at heart, you might want a song deck dedicated to songs about love and loss. The theme could be broad, covering all aspects of love, or focused on just one aspect, such as marriage, breakups, breakthroughs, or opening yourself to love, once again.

Perhaps you love dreams and shadow play. In that case, you would likely benefit from a very Scorpionic deck, with sounds and songs dealing with sex, death, dreaming, transmutation, and money. My Very Scorpio deck is for when I need my truth to sting. Every song feels like it pulls poison out and is medicine for the deep, dark places that yearn to enter the light.

Creating Your Song Deck

1 . Create a name for your first song deck and then go through all of your *Spotify (*or other music service) favorites and add as many as you wish in an intuitive fashion.

2 . Ask a friend to create a playlist or deck. I curated a list of song decks from some of my favorite creators, healers, musicians, oracle deck creators, writers, and wild hearts. Go to www.thenewromant-icsoracle.com to follow along on some of those decks.

3 . One of my favorite ways to create a song deck is through the ‹oracular algorithm› method. You begin by selecting a ‹seed song,› chosen in whatever way feels right to you. Then, on Spotify, you create a radio station from that seed song by clicking the three dots on the top right and selecting ‹go to radio.› If you›re using a different platform, you would do something similar to create an intuitive radio station based on the seed song. Finally, you save each song that plays or resonates with you, creating a playlist that becomes your divinely channeled song oracle, or song deck.

The creation of your song decks can happen slowly over time or in one marathon music selection. You can also have a deck that begins with a few dozen songs and morphs into thousands like mine has. Feel free to channel my inner teenager who spent hours looking over what C Ds she wanted to order. This deck is yours and it needs to feel like it came from your heart. Aim for each song deck to feel like you have created your own custom oracle cards in musical format. The sky is simply the start, not the limit when it comes to this type of sound divination system. A playful spirit with what I have outlined will yield the best results and the most room for the song oracle to grow and evolve as you do.

Once you've got your deck or decks—those divinely selected playlists—you're all set to chat with the song oracle. Formulate a question or use the recommended For The Record oracle cards and let the magic unfold!

If you want to see this entire process in action sign up for insider tips at www.thenewromanticsoracle.com

"Music is the language of the spirit.

It opens the secret of life, bringing peace,

abolishing strife."

–Kahlil Gibran

THE ART OF ASKING

The way we form a question is also a window into how we see life. Although there are no hard and fast rules for what you can ask the song oracle I have witnessed that the best successes are granted to those who form amazingly uplifting questions. What defines an exceptional question? Typically, one that is open-ended and empowers you to take control of your life's direction.

Here are a few examples of excellent questions:
Instead of asking, "Will I get this job?" inquire, "What qualities can I display to make me the top candidate for the position?" Rather than focusing on others, ask questions that empower you to influence outcomes. For example, instead of wondering, "Does this person like me?" consider asking, "What is the frequency/energy shared between us?" Keep your questions focused on the present moment and approach them with creativity.

Here are some questions that I often use:
1. What simple message do I need to hear today?
2. What is the biggest influence on my life right now?
3. What deserves my focus today?
4. What is my superpower for today, or this week, or this month? (Choose an interval that feels relevant to you.)
5. How can I open myself to partnership?
6. What barrier have I created in opening myself to love?

7. What is the most effective way for me to comprehend and address this challenge within my friendship or partnership?
8. What can I focus on to expand my potential in _ _ _ _ _ _ ?
9. What actions can I take right now to increase money in my life?
10. How can I bring about more healing in my body?

Now form a question, list of questions, or pull a card from the For The Record deck (sold separately) to form a question.

The next step is simple: All you have to do is turn your playlist onto shuffle, set your intention, and get ready for your divinely channeled song oracle messages.

Before you hit play or shuffle, take a moment and ask for the energy of your question to be clearly communicated through which song or songs play. Science has shown us that our attention to something changes it. We become quantumly entangled with it.

The ‹oracular algorithm› is a now responding to you and creating a feedback loop of information. This same musical algorithm can be used to ask questions of people on the other side or invisible energies that flow all around us. I will wager a guess and say, If you are reading this guidebook about musical divination you are open to life being much more strange and interesting than the news channels will ever report.

If you are using For The Record cards you will separate the deck into two piles; Side A is a series of powerful questions you can personalize, Side B gives you music selections to add to your song deck. The wild cards are just that, wild cards to spice up your song oracle session.

If you aren't working with my deck of cards, my suggestion is to look for your answer in 1-3 songs and then move on to another question. Similarly, when you work with Tarot or oracle cards, you can often find a great deal of information in one card, but sometimes you need a few clarity cards. Think of the sound oracle in the same way. Aim for simplicity and listen to follow-up songs for clarity. As always, life is a pick-your-adventure game that is about taking what you can and leaving the rest.

at the root of all power and motion there is music and rhythm. before we make music, music makes us.

Joachim-Ernst Berendt

SONG INTERPRETATION

Perspectives on life vary as uniquely as the kaleidoscope of individuals experiencing it. Each of us can watch the same movie and
focus on or notice certain things that others would not. Ultimately,
we are the meaning-makers of our own narratives. Life isn't happening to you, you are happening to life.

My biggest tip for interpretation and life: Bring your focus more
on the beauty and truth of what you find at any given moment.
Glass half-full energy. We do live in an archetypal mythical existence that mirrors our inner beliefs back to us constantly. We are
self fulfilling prophecies and what you focus on expands, so use
your energy wisely.

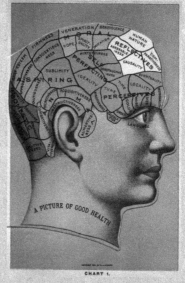

QUICK START GUIDE
(for my people who love quickies)

The New Romantics

1.  Grab your music player or connect to a streaming service.

2.  Create a song deck by gathering 30-50 songs in a oracle playlist.

3  Clean your energetic field and ask an uplifting question.

4. Hit shuffle and receive your answer in the first 1 - 3 songs. Listen for tingles and 'aha' feelings that bubble up. Remember bread crumbs may be in the album art.

5.  **SCAN ME** For my people who like it slower and more thorough watch me guide you through the entire process.

97

The collective unconscious
consists of the sum of the
instincts and their
correlates, the archetypes.
Just as everybody possesses
instincts, so he also
possesses a stock of
archetypal images.
Carl Jung

When I say "archetypal-mythical-existence" I mean the universal symbols or patterns deeply embedded within the human psyche, representing fundamental aspects of the human experience and collective unconscious, illuminating our behaviors, motivations, and recurring themes in storytelling, music, and culture.

The website Literary Terms says, "The most famous example of an archetype is the Hero. Hero stories have certain elements in common – heroes generally start out in ordinary circumstances, are "called to adventure," and in the end must confront their darkest fear in a conflict that deeply transforms the hero."

The heroine's journey, as outlined by Maureen Murdock, shares certain touchstones with the hero's journey and can be found in the archetypes of goddesses like Kali, Oshun, and Kwan Yin, each embodying different energetic signatures of the same journey of womanhood. Writer Joseph Campbell who really anchored the Hero's journey into Western society said "Women don't need to make the journey. In the whole mythological tradition, the woman is [already] there. All she has to do is to realize that she's the place that people are trying to get to."

Interpreting the songs you receive will sometimes use the same inner knowing that you would use to give meaning to a dream, or look for the deeper messages in a myth or fairytale. Some songs are clear as day and simple to interpret. No two interpretations will be the same even if you and a friend both received the same song prompted by the same question.

The New Romantics interpretation process includes using all elements of the song and in particular how the wise oracle of your body feels receiving the song. In this form of divination, there is no book; you are the living, breathing interpretation guidebook!

If you are using Spotify or a similar streaming service the interpretative process is as follows. If you aren't using a streaming music site you can adapt the process as you see fit.

the steps

First, check in with how you feel when you hear the song begin to play. Does the song elicit a strong initial response? Does the song remind you of another song that may have a clue? Does the song bring you back to a time that hints at answering your question? Begin to take stock of your initial feelings. Sometimes the song immediately resonates, and you intuitively know why it's playing. A clear insight or message may present itself.

If this is your experience you can also begin to look for and receive more information about your song selection through:

• Contemplating the lyrics as a whole.
• Noticing what you feel (resistance, opening, realization, curiosity, deep inner-knowing).
• Bring the album art and other elements of the song, which I will
expound upon further below, into the overall picture.

I invite you to take mental notes or write down your impressions
in a dedicated notebook or the provided music notes section of this
book.

Next, continue your interruption by looking at the imagery on
the album cover or the title of the song. There are often important clues in the album art and at times can contain the bulk of the
information that you will use to gather the answer to your query.
Perhaps the imagery or words point you to a conclusion or hint at
another clue in finding meaning in your song. You may also de-
cide to use elements of numerology by looking at the length of the
song or the time the song played. Use your favorite search engine
to find clues about numerology in your song reading.

I noted before that what separates a mediocre mind and a ge-
nius-level mind is how many dots one can connect. So go wild or
keep it simple, the choice is yours. My suggestion is to keep it

simple in the beginning as you are learning to trust yourself and the system. As you grow confidence in the process you can add more bells and whistles and connect dots on various levels.

Most often, I find the answer in the song title or lyrics. If it's truly a grand slam, I glean something from each level of contemplation.

TO RECAP:

1. Check the song title or album name for clues.
2. Listen closely to the lyrics.
3. Check in with your body and intuition. What are you feeling as you listen to the song?
4. Look for more deeply embedded clues such as numerology and connections to other songs or memories that might be exposed.

Music has a way of living in the recesses of our minds and can connect us to long forgotten memories. Check out my personal interpretation examples for inspiration on how to read your own songs.

Question: What do I need to most know about the Scorpio Eclipse season as it relates to my destiny?

My first impression was from the title of the song: Know What I Want by Kali Uchis. I have been in a season of exploring and getting all kinds of nudges to get clear about what I want so I know what direction to drive in. The lyrics say:

They say one door opens when another door close
I'm prayin' that's that way that it goes
'Cause right when I'm 'bout to turn the doorknob
It seems it's all locked up and the key decomposed
Remind me this the life that I chose

Kali Uchis goes on to sing "I know what I want" and that is the type of clarity I am calling in at this time.

My main song deck now has 4,346 songs to pull from and this song, although simple, felt like a grand slam. I didn't need to look for additional clues or try to read too deeply because the theme of the song and the first verse very clearly gave me the message I needed to hear. Even the car in the album art fits the analogy I have been using of G P S and picking a direction and following it.

If you work with Tarot or oracle cards you probably know that sometimes you pick a card and it doesn't make sense until weeks later when you have had time to sit with yourself. The song oracle is pulling from a finite playlist and always does its best to answer your question. Sometimes that looks like an image or two words out of all the lyrics. Use the science of chills to know what your message is, and leave the rest.

Let's look at another sample reading as a guide.

My request: "Please give me a song to ease my heart about falling in love as a flawed human being who fears if their worst thing or most ugly shadow is revealed no one will want them." A pretty universal but relevant fear guided this session with the song oracle.

My song was Fall in Love with You by Montell Fish and the first line is a falsetto voice swooning. "Fall, in love with you, you."

To me, this was a simple reminder of the main work that needs to be done in relationships. Falling in love with yourself and staying in love with oneself is the essential ingredient in being willing to open up to another, flaws and all.

This was another easy straightforward reading. I simply played it over and over again like a mantra for the rest of the night.

The special ingredient that will yield the best results over and over again is your ability to suspend disbelief and act with a child-like heart. Curiosity is the energy of inner radiance. It is the divine child within. It flows from a place of balanced light and dark. It is immense and available to everyone in equal measure.

When you are remembering curiosity and creativity you are saying to the universe I am open. I am willing to see life differently by releasing the past and being a vessel to what new information is streaming in right now. If you can come into this energetic space of curiosity and creativity the song oracle works at one of its highest vibratory states.

I personally believe the energy of the oracle is always working. You can be gutted, tired, angry, horny, or perfectly balanced and you will get back very important sound information based on your frequency and what you most need to hear.

There is no wrong way to do it. I simply offer my experience as a way to find your true note with the sound oracle. Your unique story will be the lens through which interpretation flows and the songs know that.

What to do when you don't resonate or aren't sure how to interpret.

Sometimes the song you get will leave you feeling more puzzled than settled. Sometimes, just like in life, we ask for something, and it's right in front of our faces and we still can't see it.

When this happens you can ask for a clarification song which simply means you can hit the shuffle button again or continue to let the oracle algorithm choose the next few songs to help bring clarity to your question. My sweet spot is 3 songs per question unless you are in ceremonial mode with the music.

You can also get more curious and re-listen to the song for clues that you may have missed the first time around. Sometimes the closest match or most accurate song find is based on just the artwork or title and is less lyrically driven. This is where you must use the power of your personal oracle to zone in on what's for you and leave the rest. This aspect of the process is akin to a fine art, improving with practice, much like honing your intuition—it's a muscle. Let's all flex it together!

The next track will show you how to go into ceremonial mode with sound, how to communicate with relatives or energies on the other side, as well as how to sprinkle tons of magic on the basic process outlined in this track. The system is simple but the results and the ways to make it your own are never-ending.

David Bowie
Heroes

track 05.

creativity in seeking the unseen

The song oracle music system is simple yet profound. The tools I will share in this track for creativity and interpretation breathe life into it, infusing it with flesh and bones, a heart, a pulse, and, most importantly, a soul.

Soul is what we feel when the music hits us just the right way. Soul is required for all things that want to touch the heart. Soul is the reason this system even exists.

THE SONG ORACLE GOES 'SIDEWALK ORACLE'

One of my first suggestions on how to get creative is to widen your scope beyond the song oracle deck system into the sounds of nature and the songs that happen to be playing in the places you frequent or the places you have to go on any given day. The universe loves a playful spirit and will respond in kind.

The sidewalk oracle uses any and everything they find in their path as a messenger. To use the song oracle this way you would ask your question(s) and wait for life to bring a song or a sound or go in search of your sounds and songs. Heading into the stream of synchronicity outside your comfortable bubble always yields magical results. You can play this game in airports, at the gym, doctor's office, or any other place where music is prominent.

The way to use the song oracle in this fashion is to make a request, ask a question, or set an intention and ask that a song be sent to you in a random fashion and wait until you hear your answer. I do this by setting a series of reminders on my phone. That way I don't forget the intention or question asked. You can even experiment with saying "The next song I hear on a commercial will be a direct answer to the question or intention set forth". Let life surprise you!

The frequency of sound is intuitive, creative, and fine-tuned to your asking. Your personal and unique sound oracle can take you as far (e.g. song mediumship) or near (e.g. practical advice and wisdom) as you want to go.

Across The Veil

One of my favorite things to do with the song oracle is speak to my loved ones on the other side. At first, it was just with my Mother as she is the closest person to me who has gone through the death transition.

I was able to further test my hypothesis of how easy it was to speak with souls without bodies through the song oracle during the tragic death of my former sister-in-law who died suddenly after a long battle with mental illness. She played two very specific songs to me the day she passed that both dealt with the very heavy subject of suicide.

The first song that played was one I don't even remember adding to my deck of songs. It was called Stars and Moons by an artist named Dizzy. The album art showed a woman floating into the sky and the lyrics were chilling.

Found you in the bedroom
Vacant, set in gloom
Jamming all your fingertips into all your wounds
Baby, it's a dog day
Don't you let it rule
Cause I could hold your whole weight
If you asked me to
I am starting to see stars and moons
(It's an awful sham, but I follow suit)
This is how it ends, a courageous boom

The next song is a well-known song that also includes lyrics about suicide. These two songs together left me with no doubt that I was indeed connecting beyond the veil.

Mamaaa,
Just killed a man,
Put a gun against his head, pulled my trigger,
Now he's dead
Mamaaa, life had just begun,
But now I've gone and thrown it all away

Mama, oooh,
Didn't mean to make you cry,
If I'm not back again this time tomorrow,
Carry on, carry on as if nothing really matters
Too late, my time has come,
Sends shivers down my spine, body's aching all
The time
Goodbye, everybody, I've got to go,
Gotta leave you all behind and face the truth
Mama, oooh
I don't want to die,
I sometimes wish I'd never been born at all.

My Mom who passed nearly 10 years ago sent this song to explain
to me how death was after I asked her and pressed shuffle on my
sound oracle. The gritty voice of Edward Sharpe and The Mag-
netic Zeros was her chosen song to describe the process of death.
These are the lyrics that stood out to me.

Uncomfortable,
you got to get uncomfortable
Uncomfortable,
you got to get uncomfortable

My mama was a Capricorn and a very no-nonsense, straight-up type of person, and this song made perfect sense to me while soothing my heart because we have all experienced and lived through discomfort in our lives.

No longer do we have to have an intermediary in the world of mediumship, which is the practice of "communication between spirits of the dead and living human beings." Practitioners are known as "mediums" or "spirit mediums."

If communication with the other side is something that interests you the song oracle is a great way to begin connecting with loved ones on the other side.

I recently tried this with a friend who lost a pet and she found the lyrics from 'All Is Love by Karen O from "Where the Wild Things Are" a very comforting and timely message from her beloved dog who passed away.

Do you have someone with whom you wish to communicate through the magic of the song oracle? I can attest from personal experience that using the song oracle to connect directly with my Mother, who has passed away, is one of the most powerful and healing processes. The songs create a much deeper belief in life beyond death. Each song she sends me strengthens my conviction about the afterlife and often confirms past conversations or things she has said to me. Ultimately, I encourage you to let your spirit guide you into a new and deeper conversation about how you use sound as an oracle. If this area feels dark or uncomfortable you do not have to use the sound oracle in this way. You can simply stick to issues you are facing in the here and now.

LET YOUR PROCESS BE PLAYFUL

The oracle deck I crafted to complement this guidebook is called For The Record. It delves deeper into the potential of this particular oracle system. Each card in the deck presents a challenge, a question, or a prompt designed to guide your interaction with the song deck you've crafted. If you do not have the oracle deck and want to work closer with the system, it is available on my website at www.thenewromanticsoracle.com

I also recommend having some blank note cards where you can write notes about each of your readings. I would include the date, time, song selection, phase of the moon (if you work with that sort of thing), interpretation of the song on the note card, and anything else that feels juicy and true. You can save these or toss them after they have served their divine purpose. There is always more potent magic when paper and pen touch.

Another easy way to up the creative ante in your readings is to make your own musical spreads. Spreads are an intentional layout of the ‹song cards› where each placement represents an answer to a question. In Tarot, the best-known spread is called the Celtic Cross, and it consists of 10 cards laid out in a cross shape with each card representing a different angle of the question to consider.

Spreads are a fun way to go deeper into the song oracle process. You can create a "future me" spread, your own version of the Celtic cross, or a classic 3-card/song past, present, or future spread. Get super creative! I have created several special spreads, including "The New Romantics," a remix of the Celtic Cross spread, available in the accompanying oracle deck.

MY GOD HAS A TELEPHONE   THE FLYING STARS OF BROOKLYN NY

Just like any other oracle system, your energy is your currency and point of attraction. Your aura contains a wealth of information that is readable well beyond your body. Do yourself a favor and look into HeartMath, the work of Dr. Joe Dispenza, Eileen McKusick, or ask me about my favorite frequency healing technology, like Healy, by opening this QR code. We have many direct lines to Source.

At times, we yearn to transcend the ordinary and embrace the enchanting. Rituals serve as a gateway, ushering us into a deeper connection with all of life. The song oracle system requires no special dogma or protocol but I recommend coming into your heart before you work with this or any divination tool. The heart collapses difference and polarity whereas the mind sorts, judges, and believes it is separate. The mind isn't wrong, it only has a limited view whereas the heart has the most expansive view and frequency range that can be measured. Operating within the quantum realm frees one from the constraints of conventional laws, contributing to the enigmatic and the potent nature of divination. Instead of "cause and effect" we use this powerful space to **CAUSE AN EFFECT.**

Here are a few ways to prepare yourself to receive information from the oracle.

1. A quick moment of breath with this easy mantra:
May the song I hear bring clarity. May I be able to take away a simple direct message. And so it is. Now you are ready to hit the shuffle button. You can also create a hand gesture or breath pattern that fully encompasses your prayer or desire for information. It's about wholehearted intention and less about doing things in a perfect way.

2. Pull on your spiritual lineage or things you know work well to shift the energy from the head to the vastness of the heart.

3. Ritually cleanse the area with your favorite cleansing herbs. I find Palo Santo to be the right mixture of sweet and woodsy. I use it to clear my space for a ceremonial sound session when I want to dive deeper into an issue, concern, or creative challenge.

Here are the steps I use in the ceremonial song sessions:

1. Cleanse the space.
2. Clarify my intention and have a notebook, For The Record oracle deck, or a list of questions or concerns that each card/song can address.
3. Seek assistance: from both unseen and seen allies (refer to my prayer on the following page).
4. Express gratitude in advance.
5. Hit shuffle and receive the answers.
6. Allow the interpretation to flow in with ease.
7. Thank the elements, the song oracle, and yourself. Close the space with a sound or an O M.

Prayer: I now come into perfect wholeness and stillness with a grateful heart. I now seek the answers that live all around me and within me. I trust I will be shown something that will give me insight and wisdom. I make adjustments that will better my life and all of those who interact with me. Thank you! And so it is.

the whole universe is humming.
actually, the whole universe
is mongolian throat singing.
every star, every planet, every
continent, every building,
every person is vibrating to
the slow cosmic beat. -adam frank

track 06.

Inspired
Flight
It's The
Chemicals

(outro) living as a seer

This guidebook and oracle deck are my gift to the world, a mixtape of my heart. A way to work with music as an intelligent energy of aliveness, as well as a tried-and-true, oracle system. My bright hope is that you begin to see and experience yourself as the living oracle, capable of intuitive mastery with or without the medium of music or tools, using nothing but your body and your extra sensory perceptions. This is your birthright! Each of us has an intuitive sound, a true note, that rings with absolute clarity and is capable of knowing the seemingly unknowable.

You embody music: your breath, the sounds your body produces, your voice—all form a frequency, a personal radio station broadcasting mantras and words unseen but carried in your auric field. These invisible signals actively form every moment of your life, attracting and repelling things around you.

Living as the oracle is an invitation to continually be in the process of emerging and reimagining. Releasing old stories and mindsets in favor of something fresh and always happening, yet unchanging.

Deliberately positioning yourself within the current of synchronicity allows the hand of providence to steer you towards embracing the romanticism of life and exploring beyond mere logic. It is an ongoing courtship with your inner child who always remembers the magic and the secret doors hidden in plain sight amongst us.

"Synchronicity is the transmission of messages from the world behind the world, which may include written words, or words of speech overhead, or a song that comes on the radio, or a dream image showing up in waking life, accompanied by a larger energy of recognition that may feel otherworldly."

—valley Reed

There is a word in Ireland called vaguing, which Robert Moss writes about in his book 'The Sidewalk Oracle.' "On a country walk, when you come to a fork in the road, you let your body choose which way to go. You will notice that a foot or a leg has a tendency to turn left instead of right, or the other way around, and off you go."

Can you allow your soul to choose the direction your feet take today? Can you set aside your thinking brain and feel your way into something melodious, magical, and mysterious?

The heart and soul of this book originates from an inherent openness in perceiving life and its boundless possibilities. It's a viewpoint that encourages being present, sensing the vibrant essence beneath the surface of life. New Romantics embody a spirited vitality—a curiosity that sparks the willingness to momentarily let go of skepticism, inviting magic to unfold.

123

One of my personal oracles is Julia Cameron, stoker of creative flames. She wrote the cult classic "The Artist's Way" which was her simple process for helping people remember their way as creatives and seers of all sorts. She believed all humans possessed a spirit of creation. In her book, she shares some basic foundations of creativity that I find reconnect us to the oracle within.

here are my favorites

1 . Creativity is the natural order of life. Life is energy: pure creative energy.

2 . As we open our creative channel to the creator, many gentle but powerful changes are to be expected.

3 . The refusal to be creative is self-will and counter to our true nature.

4 . Our creative dreams and yearnings come from a divine source, as we move toward our dreams, we move toward our divinity.

Julia Cameron moved toward her yearnings and created an iconic book that outlined creativity in a way that had not been done before. Her willingness to be the oracle created a book and system that has changed the lives and trajectories of over 5 million people.

Living as the oracle is my continual and deepest invitation to you. It involves opening to the energy of creativity, which is the impulse of life to grow, and transform into higher and higher levels of order and simultaneous mystery.

You Are The Oracle

The oracle sees opportunity in every morsel of life. Answers can be found on gum wrappers, billboards, in the lyrics of a song that is blaring as you ride your bike, a deep knowing in your gut, or as a download you received in a dream. The oracle understands that life provides a mirror for your own expansion, growth, and guidance. The life of a romantic is sweet, even when it is salty. The romantic has embodied the oracle energy, which knows deeply how intertwined we are with all of nature. Pull one thread, and you will find it connected to all things. The oracle fervently believes we are never alone and always have the support of the invisible realms, ready to shapeshift into whatever experience or song we need to continue awakening.

Unus Mundus is the secret code word for this romantic deep inner knowing.

"The great Second Hermetic Principle embodies the truth that there is a harmony, agreement, and correspondence between the several planes of Manifestation, Life and Being. This truth is a truth because all that is included in the Universe emanates from the same source, and the same laws, principles, and characteristics apply to each unit, or combination of units of activity, as each manifests its own phenomena upon its own plane." -The Kybalion, William Walker Atkinson

I believe Undus Mudus is what is birthed if science, spirituality, myth, and belief all merged together. A unified field of information that holds phenomena like synchronicity, divination, the collective unconscious, and pre-cognition gently in the womb of creation. The mundane and the magic intertwine to birth something superhuman. Like a membrane for the energy of creation to flow, magic will follow and show you her secrets if you but believe. The universe has its hand outstretched to you in a romantic gesture of shared evolving.

126

As the final notes of our
exploration fade, may
you carry with you
the wisdom of the
ancients and the
enchantment of
the Romantics,
allowing the rhythms of
your own life to be
guided by the eternal
music of the cosmos.

THE

POWER OF SOUND

"Every day we walk amongst things that are hidden—concealed from our immediate sensory perception. Things that nestle just along our peripheral edge like a distant buoy floating on the horizon. As human beings, we walk through our days bombarded by stimuli of all natures; our eyes, ears, noses, and mouths do all they can to give us an idea of just what is surrounding us, but a good deal gets lost in translation. So much of this missed detail is not our fault, rather an unavoidable consequence of having more to do than sit in silent absorbance of our environment. And thus, things become hidden."
Kevin McMahon

THE SECRET CHAPTER :
ROMANCE & REVERIE

WALKING AMONGST HIDDEN THINGS

Like explorers of a forgotten world, we tread softly, guided by a whisper of melody, a subtle shift in rhythm, or a cryptic clue...

Here, amidst the harmonies and cadences, lies a secret, a treasure waiting to be unearthed—a song that defies the boundaries of convention. In the realm of music, such hidden gems are not mere accidents but deliberate acts of artistry. They are the secret songs, concealed within the grooves of albums and the silence between tracks, known to only the most devoted listeners. Just like esoteric wisdom these clandestine compositions are an invitation to delve deeper, to explore the magic doorways that can go undetected but are portals for deeper knowing.

In this ethereal landscape, we shall journey together, as we touch the mysteries of secrets hidden in plain sight. We shall listen with more than just our ears, for hidden within these melodies are stories untold, emotions unspoken, and messages meant only for the most keen listeners. Let us embark on this dual quest to uncover the hidden harmonies in everyday life while we celebrate the artists who chose to share their secret tracks with the special kind of listener who follows the breadcrumbs.

Just as a hidden track nestles within an album's fallow space, so to do esoteric truths dwell in plain sight. They are the cryptic messages of the universe, waiting for those with eyes to see and hearts to understand. These esoteric truths, like the ones within these pages, or the concealed notes of a song, are there for the attentive seeker, beckoning us to decode their deeper meaning.

My wish is to present this secret track as a way to continue to connect the dots between the seen and unseen realms, to unveil some of the enigmas that surround us, for in the mundane, we may discover the most extraordinary of truths: you are the instrument through which spirit plays the symphony of life.

Before I share some of my favorite secret songs let's explore how hidden tracks began, then I'll share some of my favorite secret songs for you to add to your own musical repertoire.

The history of documented secret tracks began not that long ago with some blokes from Liverpool. The Beatles wrote a lot more music than they could fit on the album Abbey Road. Paul McCartney made the decision to cut a short acoustic piece, but his engineer, Geoff Emerick, had big balls and other plans, so he hid a track at the end of the album after a few seconds of silence. In that moment and with that tiny act of imagination and deviance, secret tracks, hidden tracks, or musical easter eggs were born.

Wikipedia defines secret tracks as; "In the field of recorded music, a hidden track is a song or a piece of audio that has been placed on a CD, audio cassette, LP record, or other recorded medium, in such a way as to avoid detection by the casual listener."

Although secret tracks are a bit of a relic from the past, audiophiles like me love them. That was the inspiration for me to include a secret chapter or "track" in this music oracle system. Not as easily accomplished as its musical counterpart but still a sweet surprise for those willing to keep turning pages.

Here is a list of secret songs I love. Do with them what you wish. Find the songs on YouTube and listen. Find the compact disc or vinyl record and resurrect your analog technology player of choice for a taste of the experience as it used to be. Get clever and figure out a way to add them to any of your song decks. Each of these songs was the gold at the end of the rainbow.

The invitation here and in hidden tracks are more than mere novelties; they are echoes of the esoteric, the unsung verses of a cosmic poem, the songs that we find playing at the perfect moment orchestrated by something intelligent and aware. They invite us to decode the universe's secret language, to decipher the rhythms of existence. They are the whispered truths, the musical mantras, that speak directly to the soul.

Secret Song Symphony

1. Tracey Chapman: New Beginnings, Save a place for me
2. Nirvana: Endless, Nameless
3. Green Day: All By Myself
4. Beach House: Wherever You Go
5. Bloc Party: Every Time Is the Last Time
6. Q-Tip: Do It, See It, Be It (Amplified)
7. Lauryn Hill: Tell Him
8. Coldplay: The Escapist
9. Yeah Yeah Yeahs: Poor Song
10. Lauryn Hill: Can't Take My Eyes Off Of You
11. The Beatles: Her Majesty

5 WAYS TO ROMANTICIZE

yourself back to life.

1. *wear something* DRAMATIC
2. *buy yourself peonies* freaking out *over them is normal they are simply heavenly*
3. *created a themed playlist that gives you* all the feels
4. *write* **the** *most* *perfect* *love letter*
5. *have* courage *my* **LOVE**

RO·MAN·TI·CIZE

to return to beauty, splendor and possibility.

WORKS CITED

7 Richard Rudd, The Gene Keys: Embracing Your Higher Purpose, Sandman Books, 2013

14 Richard Rudd, The Gene Keys: Embracing Your Higher Purpose, Sandman Books, 2013

18 Solomon Fesshaye, Save Our Place, 2022

24 Richard P. Adams, "Permutations of American Romanticism, year unknown

28 Isabella Meyer, Romanticism Art – An Overview of the Romantic Movement, 2021

29 Buckminster Fuller, Everything I Know, 1975

45 Bob Schneider, The World Exploded into Love Lonelyland, Shockorama Records, 2001

46 R. Murray Schafer, The Soundscape: Our Sonic Environment and the Tuning of the World First published January 1, 1977

46 Nathan Chandler, 10 Connections Between Physics and Music

48 Penny Wong, The universe is made up of frequency and vibration, Medium Article 2020

50 my.clevelandclinic.org/health/treatments/8817-music-therapy

51 The Science Behind Solfeggio Frequencies - BetterSleep, Dec. 2019

52 Penny Wong, The universe is made up of frequency and vibration, Medium Article 2020

56 Karl Tate, How Quantum Entanglement Works (Infographic), 2013

57 Quantum Theory Demonstrated: Observation Affects Reality, Feb. 1998, sciencedaily.com

58 Ludwig van Beethoven, 1770 - 1827

59 Arthur C. Clarke, Profiles of the Future: An Inquiry into the Limits of the Possible, 2017

62 Lian Zhu 1 and Yogesh Goyal, Art and science, EMBO Reports, 2022

63 The Gene Keys: Embracing Your Higher Purpose, 2013

65 Valerie June, Astral Plane, The Order of Time, Fantasy Records, 2017

66 Charbel Tadros, author

68 Paul O'Brien, Divination: Sacred Tools for Reading the Mind of God

73 Corinne Bailey Rae, Put Your Records, Corinne Bailey Rae, EMI, 2005

82 Plato, 429- 347 B.C.E

84 Thomas Stearns Eliot, 1888-1965

85 Madama Destiny, Written in the Stars, Music For Tarot Reading, 2020

88 Gibran Khalil Gibran, 1883-1981

95 Joachim-Ernst Berendt, 1922-2000

98 Carl Gustav Jung, 1875-1961

99 Archetype: Definition and Examples, LiteraryTerms.net

99 Articles: The Heroine's Journey, maureenmurdock.com

102 Kali Uchis, What I Want, Kali Uchis, 2014

104 Montell Fish, Fall in Love with You, Virgin, 2022

107 David Bowie, Heroes, RCA, 1977

110 Dizzy, Baby Teeth, Dizzy, 2018

111 Queen, A Night at the Opera, EM, 1975

112 All Is Love, Karen O, Where the Wild Things Are: Motion Picture
Soundtrack, Warner Brothers, 2009

120 Adam Frank, Atlantic Magazine, 2023

123 Valley Reed, Jung and the Mysteries of Wordless Transmission, 2020

121 Inspired flight ft. Scarab, It's The Chemicals, We All Want to Fly, 2010

123 Robert Moss, Sidewalk Oracles: Playing with Signs, Symbols, and Synchronicity
in Everyday Life, New World Library, 2015

126 William Walker Atkinson, The Kybalion, BookRix, 2019

144 Kevin McMahon, Len Comaratta, Brian Josephs and Katherine Flynn,
20 Best Hidden Tracks on Albums, Consequence of Sound, 2014

149 Tracey Chapman, New Beginnings, Save a place for me, Elektra, 1995

149 Nirvana, Endless, Nameless, Come As You Are, DGC, May 1991

149 Green Day, All By Myself, Fresh Meat (Live 1992), Reprise, February 1, 1994

149 Beach House: Wherever You Go, Bloom, Beach House, Car Park Records, 2012

149 Bloc Party: Every Time Is the Last Time, Silent Alarm, FrenchKiss, 2005

149 Q-Tip: Do It, See It, Be It, Amplified, Arista, 1999

149 Lauryn Hill: Tell Him, The Miseducation of Lauryn Hill, Ruffhouse Records,
1998

149 Coldplay: Viva la Vida or Death and All His Friends, EMI, 2008

149 Yeah Yeah Yeahs: Poor Song, Fever to Tell, Interscope, 2003

149 Lauryn Hill, Can't Take My Eyes Off Of You, The Miseducation of Lauryn
Hill, Ruffhouse Records, 1998

149 The Beatles, Her Majesty, Abbey Road, Sony, 1969

MAY WE KNOW OURSELVES AS
BEAUTY AND ROMANCE.

WILDROSEPUBLISHINGTX@GMAIL.COM

RECORD TEMPLATE
reg. $12 value
our price
2 for $9
MOCKUP
DIST. CORP.

Printed in the USA
CPSIA information can be obtained
at www.ICGtesting.com
LVHW070605080924
790210LV00015B/192